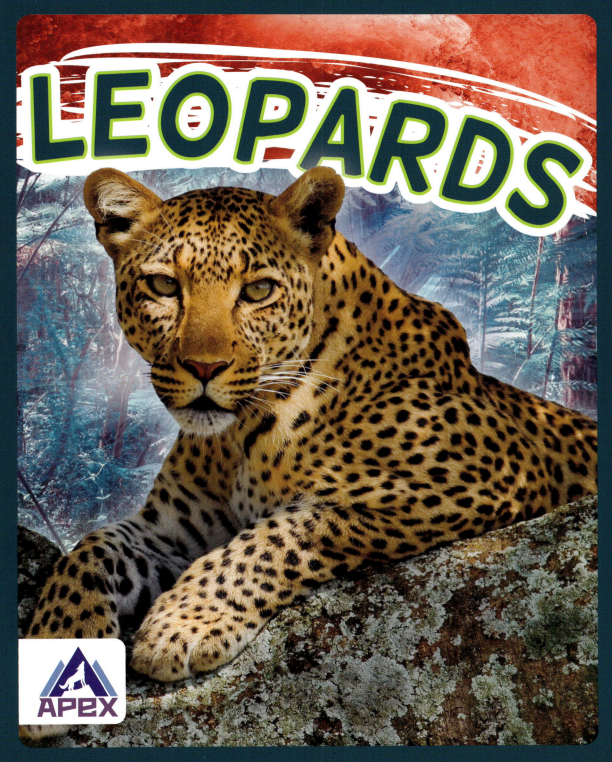

LEOPARDS

By Sophie Geister-Jones

WWW.APEXEDITIONS.COM

Copyright © 2022 by Apex Editions, Mendota Heights, MN 55120. All rights reserved. No part of this book may be reproduced or utilized in any form or by any means without written permission from the publisher.

Apex is distributed by North Star Editions:
sales@northstareditions.com | 888-417-0195

Produced for Apex by Red Line Editorial.

Photographs ©: Shutterstock Images, cover, 1, 4–5, 6–7, 8, 9, 10–11, 12–13, 14–15, 16–17, 18, 19, 20–21, 22–23, 24, 25, 26–27, 29

Library of Congress Control Number: 2020952945

ISBN
978-1-63738-031-4 (hardcover)
978-1-63738-067-3 (paperback)
978-1-63738-135-9 (ebook pdf)
978-1-63738-103-8 (hosted ebook)

Printed in the United States of America
Mankato, MN
082021

NOTE TO PARENTS AND EDUCATORS

Apex books are designed to build literacy skills in striving readers. Exciting, high-interest content attracts and holds readers' attention. The text is carefully leveled to allow students to achieve success quickly. Additional features, such as bolded glossary words for difficult terms, help build comprehension.

TABLE OF CONTENTS

CHAPTER 1
HIDDEN IN THE GRASS 5

CHAPTER 2
CLIMBING CATS 11

CHAPTER 3
SPOTS AND WHISKERS 17

CHAPTER 4
SNEAK ATTACK 23

Comprehension Questions • 28

Glossary • 30

To Learn More • 31

About the Author • 31

Index • 32

CHAPTER 1
HIDDEN IN THE GRASS

A leopard creeps through the tall grass. Her cub follows close behind. Several antelopes munch on grass up ahead.

Leopards often hunt large animals. But they also eat birds and insects.

The leopard's ears flick. Her cub stops. He settles by a tree. He watches his mother carefully. She sneaks closer to the antelopes. She **crouches** low to the ground.

SPOT TALK

Leopards have white spots on the backs of their ears and tails. These spots stick out in tall grass and leaves. Leopards use these spots to **communicate** without making noise.

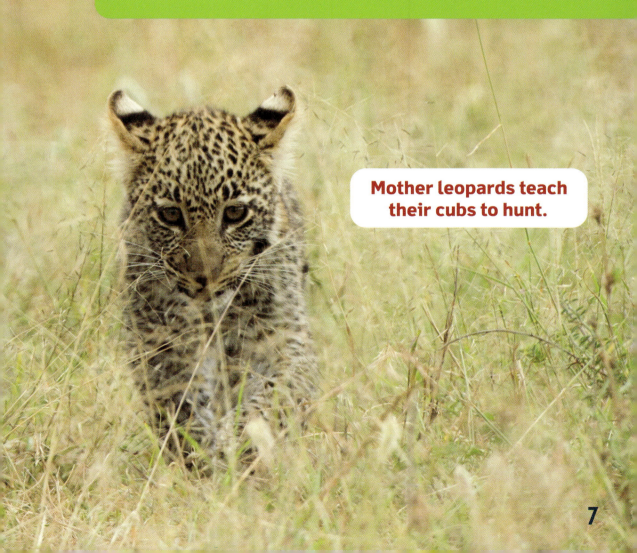

Mother leopards teach their cubs to hunt.

Then, she darts forward. The antelopes scatter. But the leopard catches one of them. Her cub runs to her. They feast.

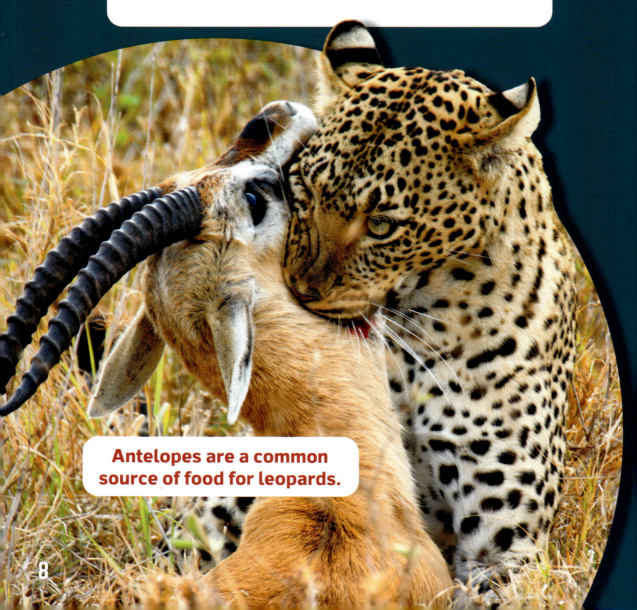

Antelopes are a common source of food for leopards.

A leopard cub stays with its mother for one to two years.

Leopards usually have two or three cubs at a time.

CHAPTER 2
CLIMBING CATS

Leopards are **adaptable** cats. They can live in many places and **climates**. Leopards often live in forests. They spend a lot of time in trees.

Leopards can be found in forests, grasslands, deserts, and mountains.

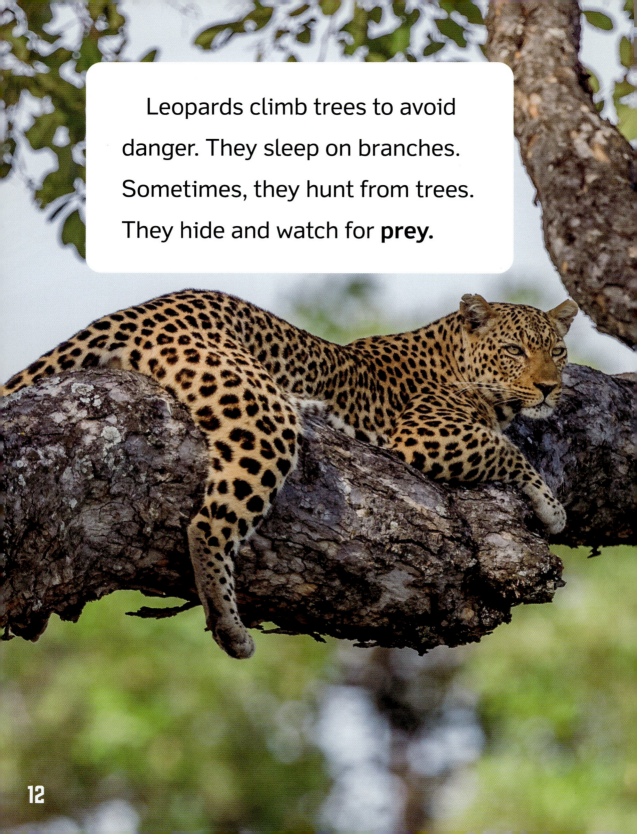

Leopards climb trees to avoid danger. They sleep on branches. Sometimes, they hunt from trees. They hide and watch for **prey.**

Up in trees, leopards are safe from bigger animals such as lions and tigers.

Leopards are strong swimmers. They sometimes catch fish.

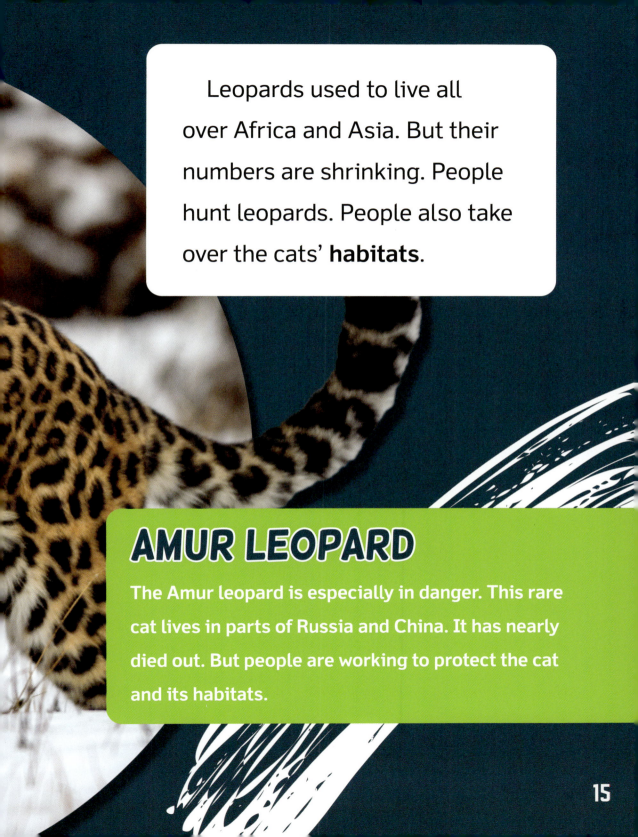

Leopards used to live all over Africa and Asia. But their numbers are shrinking. People hunt leopards. People also take over the cats' **habitats**.

AMUR LEOPARD

The Amur leopard is especially in danger. This rare cat lives in parts of Russia and China. It has nearly died out. But people are working to protect the cat and its habitats.

CHAPTER 3
SPOTS AND WHISKERS

Leopards are big cats. Some leopards can weigh 200 pounds (91 kg). Leopards have long tails. Their tails help them balance while climbing trees.

A leopard's sharp claws grip tree bark.

Leopards have yellow fur with dark spots. These spots are called rosettes. They help leopards blend in.

A leopard's spots make the cat hard to see in leaves and grass.

A jaguar has a bigger body than a leopard does.

SPOT THE DIFFERENCE

It can be hard to tell leopards and jaguars apart. Jaguars also have dark spots. But their spots have black dots in the middle. Leopards' spots do not.

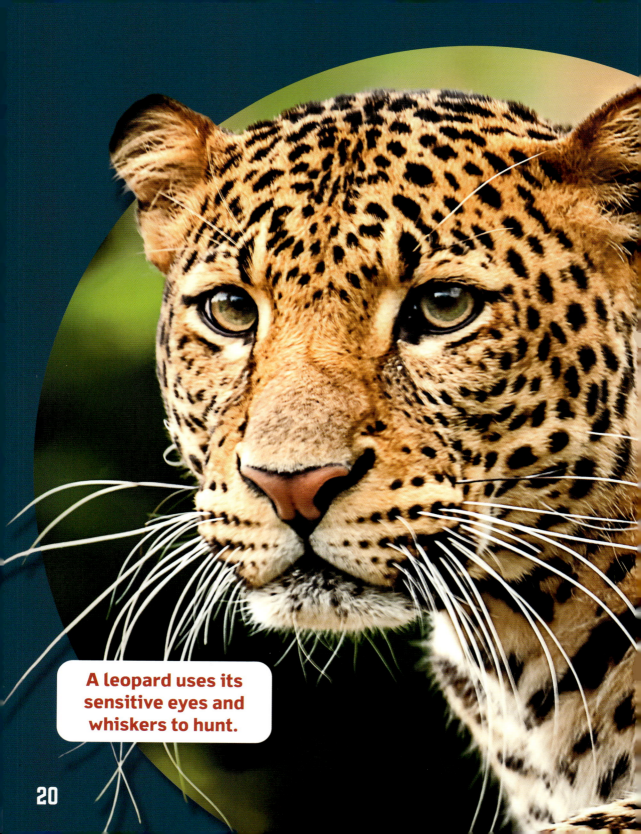

A leopard uses its sensitive eyes and whiskers to hunt.

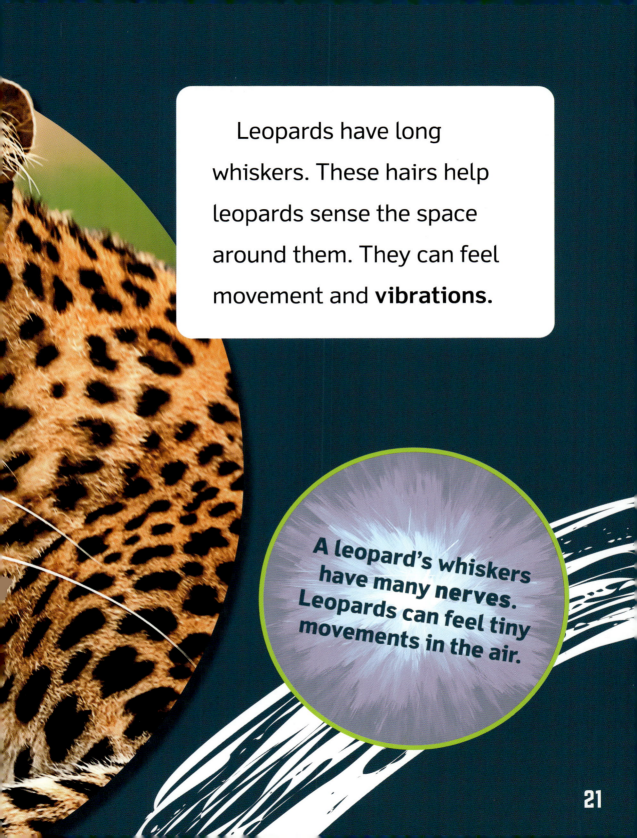

Leopards have long whiskers. These hairs help leopards sense the space around them. They can feel movement and **vibrations.**

A leopard's whiskers have many nerves. Leopards can feel tiny movements in the air.

Chapter 4
Sneak Attack

Leopards are **nocturnal**. They hunt at night. Leopards eat many different animals. They sneak up on their prey.

Leopards may eat deer, rabbits, monkeys, pigs, and more.

Leopards approach their prey slowly and quietly. When they get close, they jump. They clamp their teeth onto their prey to kill the animals.

A leopard can run 36 miles per hour (58 km/h) for a short time.

Most leopards live and hunt alone.

A leopard licks the fur off its prey before eating it.

A leopard pulls an impala up into a tree to eat it.

Next, leopards drag their catches up into trees. They may climb 50 feet (15 m) above the ground. Leopards also store leftover food in trees.

LITTLE HUNTERS

Leopard cubs practice hunting with their siblings. They **stalk** one another. Then they practice jumping. If one cub gets away, the others chase it.

Wild leopards usually live 10 to 12 years.

COMPREHENSION QUESTIONS

Write your answers on a separate piece of paper.

1. Write a sentence describing how leopards hunt their prey.

2. Leopards hunt at night. Do you prefer doing things at night or in the morning? Why?

3. What body part helps a leopard sense vibrations?
   - **A.** its tail
   - **B.** its whiskers
   - **C.** its teeth

4. What would pulling food up into trees help leopards do?
   - **A.** keep the food away from other animals
   - **B.** make the food smaller
   - **C.** catch and eat bigger animals

5. What does **rare** mean in this book?

*This **rare** cat lives in parts of Russia and China. It has nearly died out.*

    A. not in danger
    B. easy to find or see
    C. not found in large numbers

6. What does **approach** mean in this book?

*Leopards **approach** their prey slowly and quietly. When they get close, they jump.*

    A. to move toward something
    B. to move away from something
    C. to go to sleep

Answer key on page 32.

GLOSSARY

adaptable
Good at changing to fit new situations.

climates
The usual weather in certain areas.

communicate
To send and receive messages.

crouches
Bends down and stays close to the ground.

habitats
The places where animals normally live.

nerves
Long, thin fibers that carry information between the brain and other parts of the body.

nocturnal
Awake and active at night.

prey
An animal that is hunted and eaten by another animal.

stalk
To slowly and quietly sneak toward something.

vibrations
Tiny back-and-forth movements.

TO LEARN MORE

BOOKS

Markle, Sandra. *The Great Leopard Rescue: Saving the Amur Leopards*. Minneapolis: Millbrook Press, 2017.

Shaffer, Lindsay. *Snow Leopards*. Minneapolis: Bellwether Media, 2020.

Sommer, Nathan. *Gorilla vs. Leopard*. Minneapolis: Bellwether Media, 2020.

ONLINE RESOURCES

Visit **www.apexeditions.com** to find links and resources related to this title.

ABOUT THE AUTHOR

Sophie Geister-Jones lives in Saint Paul, Minnesota. She loves reading. She and her brothers have a book club.

INDEX

A
Africa, 15
Amur leopard, 15
antelopes, 5–6, 8
Asia, 15

C
climbing, 12, 17, 27
cubs, 5–6, 8–9, 27

E
ears, 6–7

F
food, 27
forests, 11
fur, 18, 25

H
habitats, 15
hunting, 12, 15, 23, 27

P
prey, 12, 23–25

S
spots, 7, 18–19
swimming, 13

T
tails, 7, 17
teeth, 24
trees, 6, 11–12, 17, 27

W
whiskers, 21

Answer Key:
1. Answers will vary; **2.** Answers will vary; **3.** B; **4.** A; **5.** C; **6.** A